LEE AND GRANT AT APPOMATTOX

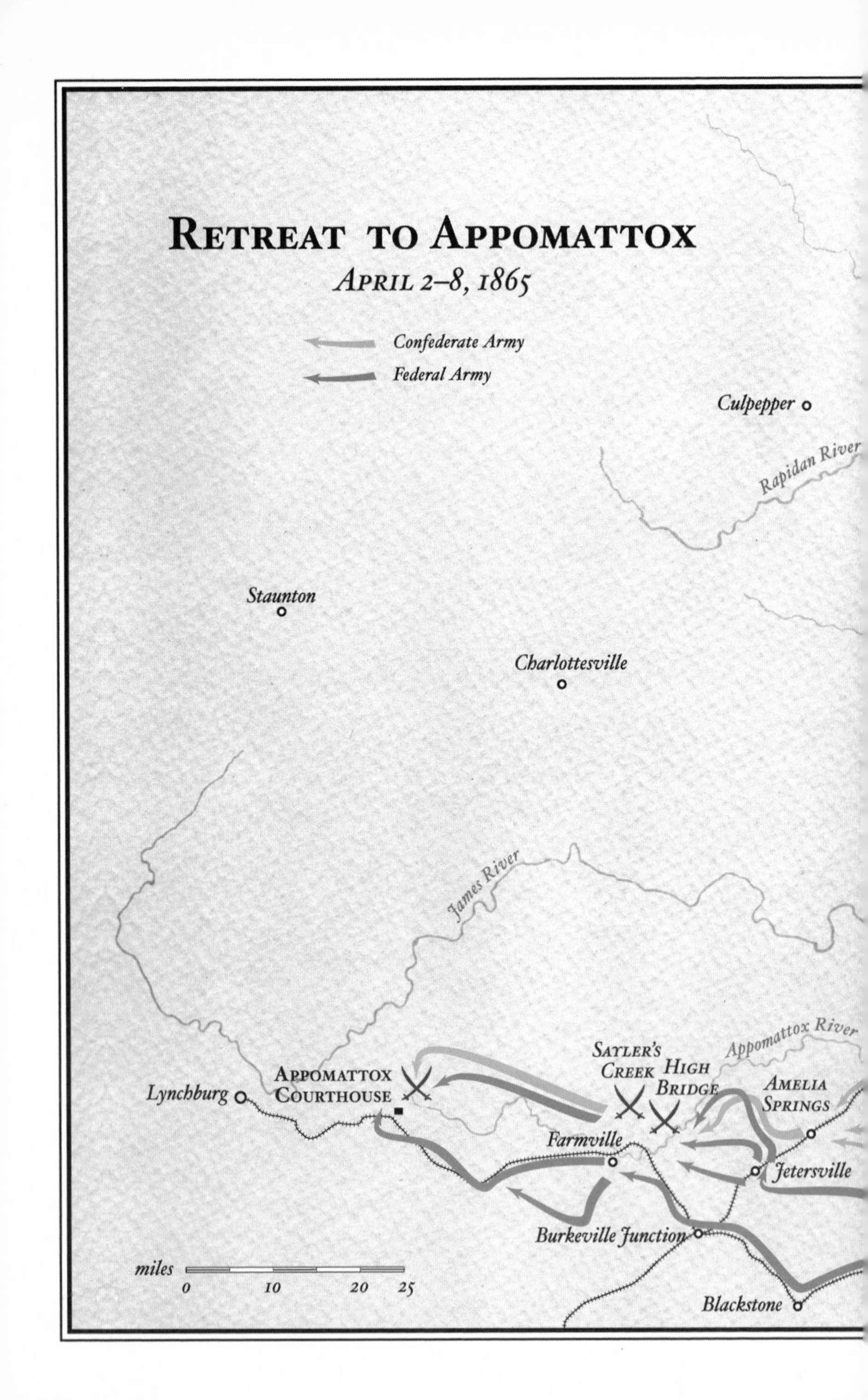
RETREAT TO APPOMATTOX
APRIL 2–8, 1865
Confederate Army
Federal Army
Culpepper
Rapidan River
Staunton
Charlottesville
James River
Appomattox River
SAYLER'S CREEK
HIGH BRIDGE
AMELIA SPRINGS
APPOMATTOX COURTHOUSE
Lynchburg
Farmville
Jetersville
Burkeville Junction
Blackstone
miles
0
10
20
25

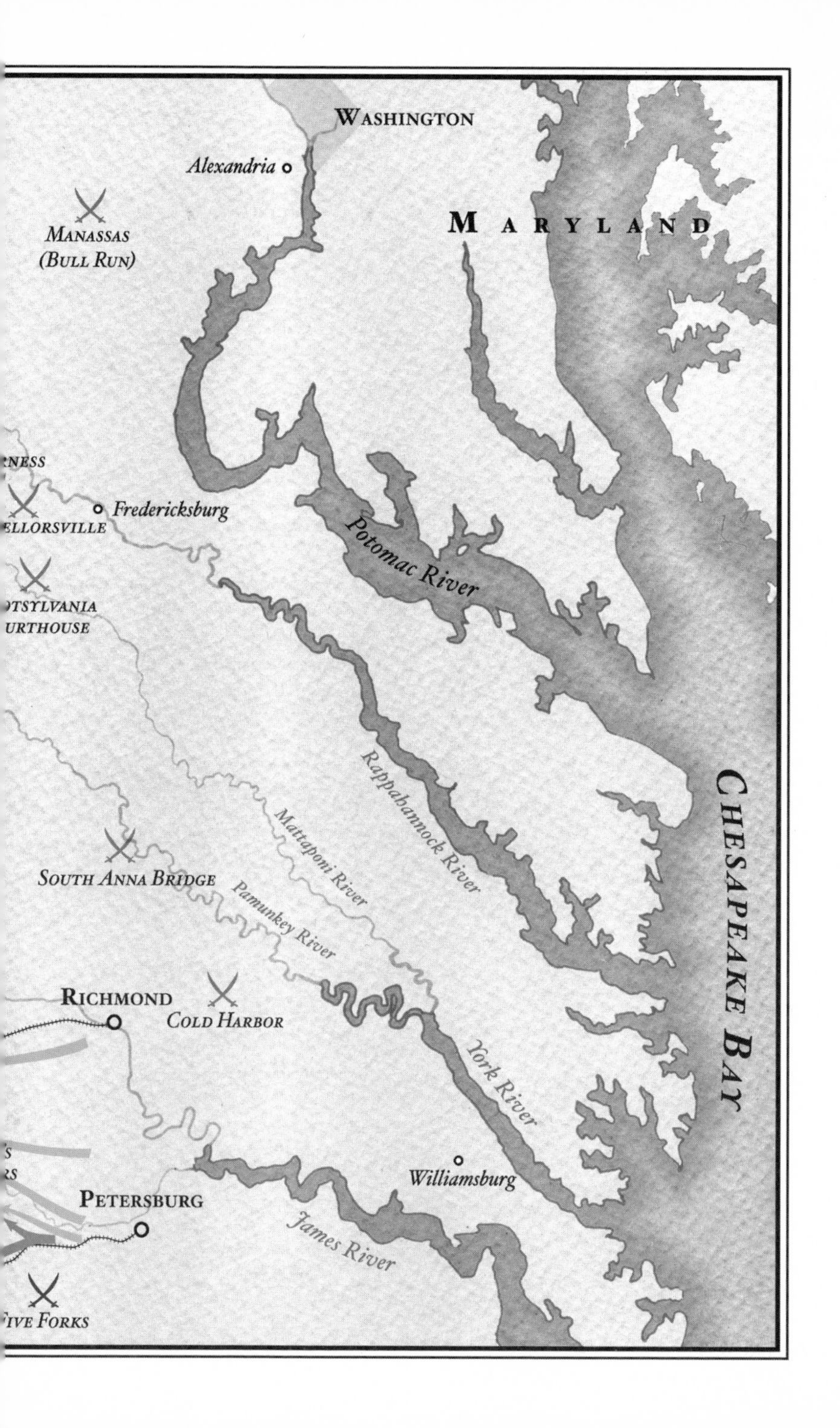

Washington
Alexandria
Maryland
Manassas (Bull Run)
Fredericksburg
Potomac River
Rappahannock River
Mattaponi River
Pamunkey River
South Anna Bridge
Richmond
Cold Harbor
York River
Williamsburg
Petersburg
James River
Chesapeake Bay

Generals Ulysses S. Grant and Robert E. Lee

LEE AND GRANT AT APPOMATTOX

MacKINLAY KANTOR

New York / London
www.sterlingpublishing.com/kids

A FLYING POINT PRESS BOOK

Design: PlutoMedia and John T. Perry III
Front cover painting: John Paul Strain
Frontispiece photographs: Corbis

Library of Congress Cataloging in Publication Data

Kantor, MacKinlay, 1904–1977.
Lee and Grant at Appomattox / MacKinlay Kantor.
p. cm. — (Sterling point books)
Originally published: New York : Random House, 1950.
ISBN-13: 978-1-4027-5124-0
ISBN-10: 1-4027-5124-9
1. Appomattox Campaign, 1865—Juvenile literature. 2. United States—History—Civil War, 1861–1865—Peace—Juvenile literature. 3. Lee, Robert E. (Robert Edward), 1807–1870—Juvenile literature. 4. Grant, Ulysses S. (Ulysses Simpson), 1822–1885—Juvenile literature. I. Title.

E477.67.K36 2007
973.7'38—dc22
2007012954

2 4 6 8 10 9 7 5 3 1

Published by Sterling Publishing Co., Inc.
387 Park Avenue South, New York, NY 10016
Original edition published by Random House

Distributed in Canada by Sterling Publishing
c/o Canadian Manda Group, 165 Dufferin Street
Toronto, Ontario, Canada M6K 3H6
Distributed in the United Kingdom by GMC Distribution Services
Castle Place, 166 High Street, Lewes, East Sussex, England BN7 1XU
Distributed in Australia by Capricorn Link (Australia) Pty. Ltd.
P.O. Box 704, Windsor, NSW 2756, Australia

Printed in China

Sterling ISBN-13: 978-1-4027-5124-0
ISBN-10: 1-4027-5124-9

For information about custom editions, special sales, premium and corporate purchases, please contact Sterling Special Sales Department at 800-805-5489 or specialsales@sterlingpub.com.

To Mary Virginia Sours

CONTENTS

FOREWORD

THE AMERICAN CIVIL WAR WAS PERHAPS the most painful experience this country has ever undergone. In 1860 the United States was growing quickly in population and expanding rapidly westward to the Pacific Ocean. The states in the North were changing most rapidly as immigrants were landing in northern cities from Europe in large numbers and factories were being built throughout New England, New York, and Pennsylvania. The South, however, remained largely farmland as it had been since before the Revolution.

Undoubtedly the biggest question of the time was over the practice of slavery. Many in the North believed that to hold men and women in slavery was wrong and immoral. The Northern states had long since given up the practice of slavery. There were few slaves in the North after the Revolutionary War and slavery was outlawed in all of the Northern states by 1804. Southerners, however, believed that it was important to own slaves to tend and harvest their crops. They felt that their way of life would be harmed without slavery. In addition, they believed that the Federal government had no right to dictate whether they could own slaves in their states.

Thus, soon after Abraham Lincoln was elected president the Southern states seceded, or broke away, from the rest of the United States, and war started between the North and the South. For almost five years the armies of the North and the South fought each other in a series of bloody battles. There were more deaths and casualties in this war than in any of our country's wars either before or since. It seemed as if this terrible war would tear the country apart permanently, no matter what the outcome of the fighting was.

This book tells the story of the moment when that great war came to an end. Ultimately, the Southern armies under General Robert E. Lee surrendered to the leader of the Union army, General Ulysses S. Grant. These great men knew how important it would be to start the healing of the nation. Not only would the terms of the surrender be important, but General Grant also realized that it would be important to treat General Lee and his beaten army with respect. This is the story of the beginning of the re-uniting of the United States.

LEE AND GRANT
AT APPOMATTOX

CHAPTER 1

BLAZING TORCHES

The constant marching and fighting without sleep or food are rapidly thinning the ranks of this grand old army. Men now fall out of ranks simply because it is beyond their power of physical endurance to go any farther.

—Southerner William Miller Owen

IT WAS BEGINNING TO GROW DARK, AND mothers called to their children. "Tom-meee! Sal-leee! Time for bed."

There were soldiers scattered all over town. Sentries stood close to the porch of the little hotel, where the general sat in a rocking chair.

The general received many dispatches, and sent more messages to his far-flung divisions, stretched like bumpy snakes along every road in the region.

Through this southcentral Virginia village of Farmville one corps of the army made its way in the April dusk, regiment after regiment, veterans all. They did not look like the stiff purple-clad men we see in fanciful old illustrations. They did not look like the smart-alec recruits they had been when they left their home towns—when local bands played "Hail, Columbia" and girls stood squealing under lacy parasols.

The troops had struggled in the line south of Richmond through chilly weeks of a dawning spring; there they had won a victory. Secessionists were now in flight; these boys in dirty blue uniforms were after them.

Flight and pursuit—if you can call it that. No one was actually running, most of the time. Half-starved men in gray, shepherded by General Lee and a thousand of his officers, stumbled and strode toward the west across pink clay ridges.

Occasionally an order was hooted aloud, occasionally some horsemen loped up through mud or dust; voices quacked shrilly. The Confederates moved aside to kneel, to hide themselves behind each clump of thin green leaves, each tangle of bleached fence rails; to poke their rifles through underbrush and wait, wait, wait until the approach of Yankee brigades made the low hills shake. Then there would be a shot, maybe a half-dozen: the scattered peppery fire of pickets, smelling ahead and falling back on the main advance.

Each time the enemies slapped out with their fire, some boys would be left sprawled amid the weeds. The soldiers in stained gray shirts and pants would rise and take up their blistered retreat again.

Union columns approached cautiously, sometimes spreading wide by companies and shooting as they came. Again the nervous flame of Confederate rifles would spit a greeting.

Once in a while some tense youngster of this shabby rear guard—not too beaten down by lack of food, by endless hours of stamp, stamp, stamping along rutted roads, not too collapsed—might puff the air out of his lungs and blow it from his throat in a high-pitched screech to be taken up by the others. "Whoooooo. . . ."

"Yes, yes," an old man said, many years later, "it was something to hear them Rebs!" The other old fellows, slouched around him on the city hall steps, would all be nodding and laughing about it. "Sonny, if you'd ever heard the Rebel Yell, you wouldn't ever forget it."

But now, no matter how the yell screeched, it was the gasp of a dying army—a broken, hungry, scabby pageant that dissolved hour by hour. Oh, they could halt the Yanks momentarily in many of these rear-guard actions. Tired ranks of dark-clad pursuers would sink to concealment amid the holly trees or along roadside ditches. Another charge might be ordered, in an attempt to dislodge the stubborn runaways. Often the Confederates would have to give ground, backing off among old corn-stubble. Sometimes they would surrender as the Northerners hustled up to them. They would hold their empty guns high in the air. A man can fight without food for a long time—thousands of them were doing it—but you can't fight without ammunition.

Sometimes, too, the patched-up butternut ranks would hold fast, and it would be the Yankees who ducked to safety. But always eventually the ragged throngs would stir again, withdraw from mossy boulders, shrink away from dead pine scrub. The retreat would continue. West, west, forever west . . . certain divisions taking advantage of side lanes, wheeling briefly to the right as they fled, and then left again into the next valley . . . back to the main road, tramping in a discouraged dream with empty haversacks, swearing to each other, wondering about the fairy-tale rations that were supposed to be awaiting them just beyond the next ridge or the next town.

Back in Farmville a sturdy man (whose last permanent address was Galena, Illinois, and whose most recent civilian occupation was that of clerk in his father's harness store) took a bruised cigar out of his pocket and sat solemnly chewing it as he watched his soldiers stringing through the gloom. He was tired, he was thinking. His staff grouped at the other end of the porch, chatting in low tones, glancing now and then toward their commander as his cigar-coal became a fat firefly in the dusk.

Another officer, one of a company passing at that moment, moved near enough to the porch to recognize the dusty booted figure with cigar thrust out from his brown beard.

The lieutenant saluted quickly, then dropped back to speak to a friend.

"Yes, that's him—over there on the porch! It's the old man . . . yes . . . Grant."

A sergeant in one of the files beyond heard the name; he looked, he told others. Young infantrymen turned their heads, gawking with curiosity. You don't often see the big boss himself in a war. Most times you never see him. He can't be everywhere at once.

"Right over there. See—in that rocking chair? That's him."

Some of the younger soldiers, weary as they were from a week of frantic chasing and battling, began to cheer. Other voices took it up; in a moment the village roadway was echoing with yelps and howls. Even the officers became infected with enthusiasm. No review had been ordered: You don't have dress parades when you are covered with dirt, as most people are always covered with dirt in a war. But this was the sort of thrill we all appreciate—the novelty, the excitement of the unexpected.

No one of these troops had thought to see his commander sitting a few yards away, smoking, watching them. Some of the tired companies responded to hasty commands: They gripped their weapons tightly, they held them at the prescribed angle, they threw out their chests, they snapped their gaze to the side.

But the joy that ruled the Federals in this hour could not be restrained by formal discipline. "Grant! Grant! . . . Yoo-hoo, Ulysses! . . . Hey, Daddy! Here I am." With the ringing sarcasm that young American soldiers bring to the grim activity of conflict and always have, they hallooed through the dusk.

News was passed to the rear. There were no walkie-talkies in those days, but by word of mouth the regiments who had not yet stepped into the street of Farmville knew soon enough that their general was on that porch and would see them pass.

Men broke away from the ranks and went clawing

amid brush on either side of the road. Pine branches, dead pine knots: Those would make good torches. They lighted whatever sticks they could get hold of. Soldiers brandished the flaming things as they fell back into the ranks or went scooting ahead to catch up with their proper squads.

The street was sparked with flame; smoke and glare and smell of the burning went aloft, faces were all ruddy with it. "Yoo-hoo, General! . . . Grant . . . Grant!" They waved their rifles, they held them straight aloft, they put their greasy caps over the muzzles as they roared.

There was every reason in the world for the troops to rejoice. If anyone spoke out severely against this madcap display of spirit, the record has been lost. The boys had fought a war; now it was nearly won. They had driven the enemy out of Petersburg, they had chased the gray-backs all week.

This was Friday, the seventh of April, 1865. It wouldn't be long now. Everybody knew it . . . Confederate stragglers crouched abjectly in the barnyards; the main army of the Secesh was only a little way ahead. Young men gabbled happily . . . the war would soon be over. Those who wanted to become bridegrooms bragged about being home and being married by May.

About three miles from this village, beyond the disordered rifle-flashes of the farthest Union advance, past a wilderness of barren unplowed fields, General Robert E. Lee sat in a farmhouse, spent and grim. He could feel his once-proud Army of Northern Virginia breaking apart.

The solemn discomfort of a tired, ravaged land rose in the evening like a mist from trampled fodder. Emptiness: hollow haymows, pens with no pigs in them, wagons with no cargoes, pouches in which only half a dozen paper-wrapped cartridges lay loosely where there should have been forty . . . exhaustion . . . hunger, hunger: always that. No biscuits to chew while marching, no pork to toast at the ramrod's tip when you lit a fire at night.

Lee was too far away to hear the hullabaloo of his enemies as they pulled their strained muscles into fresh activity, and pranced through the Farmville street, and felt the eyes of their nearly victorious chief upon them.

Flames crackled from the makeshift torches. Metal of the muskets flashed like red jewelry as the troops waved them high. "Hey, Ulysses, old fellow! . . . Hello, sir—remember me? I got shot at Cold Harbor!" That was good for a laugh any time. All too many people *had* been shot at Cold Harbor.

Children ran away from their parents and crept out of the houses to stare round-eyed at these thousands of tall, tired young men in the hated blue uniforms. Soldiers crowded the street, and more of them were filing on from behind.

Torches burned out and were tossed aside. A little boy ran close to gather up a charred branch, to sniff its smoke and wonder about it. "Grant! . . . Grant!" The general sat motionless in his rocking chair, watching them pass. His cigar was almost gone.

CHAPTER 2

GENERALS DON'T ALL LOOK ALIKE

The almost six-foot-tall, erect, impeccably dressed Lee was the exact opposite of the stubby, bearlike General Grant in most every outward way excepting a love of horses.

—Robert Hendrickson, *The Road to Appomattox*

MAYBE HIS SOLDIERS DID CALL HIM AN OLD man, but Grant was only forty-two. There was not a trace of gray in his brown beard.

At no other moment in American history might there have been such contrast between the commanders of opposing armies: Grant and Lee, preparing themselves for a few hours of rest—only three miles apart.

Grant could never have been counted a success at any time in his life until this war came along. He was the son of a tannery owner, a small businessman who had taken pride in Grant's appointment to the United States Military Academy, who had suffered grief at witnessing the ruin of his son's Army career (as all supposed) when Grant was forced in 1854 to resign his commission.

It was whiskey and nothing else that caused *that*, declared the gossips in Grant's home neighborhood. They looked at him with scorn when he came back to the Middle West, his career blasted to bits, and attempted to maintain his wife and children through various ill-starred commercial ventures. In his wife's hometown, St. Louis, it was said that folks used to cross the street in order to avoid meeting "Cap" Grant on the sidewalk. They were afraid he would try to borrow money from them.

The spring of 1861 found Grant as little better than a man living on a pension. He received a meager salary from his brothers, who conducted a harness store and hide business for their father in Galena, Illinois, but he was not admired locally. The townspeople did not even elect him captain of their militia company, the Jo Daviess Guards, whom he had helped to train in their drill.

Grandma Gratiot said in her frail old lady's voice: "Yes, I remember . . . the day the company went away to war, he was in citizen's clothes. They marched along Main Street; everybody was cheering the men in uni-

form, and Grant kept pace with them, walking along the sidewalk, carrying his carpet bag."

He was grimly determined to serve in this war. He felt that he had been educated in the art of soldiering at the nation's expense, and here was his chance to pay his debt to his country. He said as much, in a letter to Washington; he said modestly that he thought he was fit to command as much as a regiment. The authorities ignored his letter.

Grant sat for a time in an office at the Illinois State Capitol, making out various technical military forms so perplexing to the minds and eyes of civilian clerks. Here was something that he alone knew how to do.

At length an even better opportunity came his way. The colonel of one of the Illinois volunteer regiments resigned in disgust; he declared that his men were a ruffianly crew who ignored any commands given them. Grant was offered the leadership of this regiment.

There are ways of training even the most rebellious soldiers into proper behavior, and Grant knew the ways. Before long he was commanding a brigade, then a division; that was the way it went.

He campaigned along the Mississippi for nearly

three years. He captured forts considered impregnable, he broke up whole Confederate armies. His tactics might not always win the approval of wise souls who sit in offices and try to reduce battles to a formula, but they brought results.

Abraham Lincoln said, long before he ever set eyes on Grant, but when the news of victories won by the sober-faced Westerner made the only good news around Washington: "I like that man. He fights."

There used to be an old yarn about someone declaring to the President: "You can't promote Grant, Mr. President. Why, he drinks whiskey all the time!"

And Lincoln is supposed to have said: "Find out what brand of whiskey he drinks. I want to send a barrel of it to each of my other generals."

There doesn't seem to be much foundation for this story. Still, it sounds like something Lincoln might have said, and something that could have been said with truth about this silent, shabby, stubborn man who rode horseback with the skill of a Sioux Indian, who could jog for hours past bloody corpses, past tents where the wounded huddled moaning and dejected, and where other youths screamed their hearts out as surgeons hacked off their mutilated arms or legs. He could ride past sights like these and never seemingly show a quiver of pity; yet he was driven into fury if ever he saw a teamster beating his mules.

Animals seemed to count more than people, with Grant. Maybe it is necessary to be like that, if one is to squander a thousand lives through some mistake of judgment during a battle.

Except perhaps for the strange dignity of silence, Robert E. Lee resembled his opponent in no way whatsoever. Lee's people were not tanners or small storekeepers; they were aristocrats. His father was Light-Horse Harry Lee, a dashing general who won fame in the Revolutionary War. His wife was a daughter of George Washington Parke Custis, Martha Washington's own grandchild.

The Lees had always lived in aloof elegance. Robert E. Lee distinguished himself with increasing brilliance as the years went by. For some time he was superintendent of that same military academy at West Point where Ulysses Grant struggled to maintain himself as a cadet with a mere average grade. During the war with Mexico, nearly twenty years before this sad spring of 1865, Lee served in an important post on the staff of General Winfield Scott, the United States commander.

When states of the South began to secede, in the

threatening winter which preceded the firing on Fort Sumter, General Scott still commanded the troops of this nation. But he was old—very old—and so feeble that he had to be helped into his carriage. Scott must retire. He could not possibly be faced with the responsibility of commanding Northern armies in an open struggle with the South.

Men examined the records, the lists of accomplished soldiers available. The name "Lee" was spoken, even in the White House. Soon enough the command of the Federal forces was offered to Robert E. Lee of Virginia—still a colonel in the Regular Army. He was faced with a grievous decision: loyalty to his state, or loyalty to his nation?

That doesn't seem like much of a puzzle to those of us alive today in a country strongly united, with a recent history of boys from Alabama and boys from Iowa fighting side by side in three foreign wars. It would seem only amusing, now, if some man in the state of Wyoming insisted that he must support Wyoming but never the United States.

But in the nineteenth century it was far different. A hot bloody war that would hammer the wrangling commonwealths together, fuse them like metal into a solid shield: This had not occurred.

It seemed perfectly natural to hundreds of thousands of angry-eyed young fellows all over the South to give loyalty each to his individual state—never to the nation. This was the belief in which they had been nourished, and which they were ready to defend with their fists or their rifles. Wrong or right, there is no arguing it now.

Robert E. Lee declined to take command of the United States Army. He chose instead to go with his state, Virginia, when she left the Union. He fought intently through the four unhappy years that followed. He commanded the Army of Northern Virginia—the largest and most important Confederate army in the eastern portion of the country—through the great share of its successes and failures. Now he had been given supreme command of all the Confederate forces in the field.

Picture the two generals side by side, though you will not see them so until the Sunday that follows. Already you know what Grant looked like; but let your eyes brighten as they witness the grave magnificence of Lee—"Marse Robert," as his troops called him affectionately. He was nearly into old age: He had been born fifty-eight years before, yet he stood nearly six feet tall with scarcely a stoop of his fine shoulders. His face was handsome, refined, as stern and commanding as the features of a marble statue. His beard and hair were silver. You could imagine him in the wars of long ago, in polished armor. You could imagine him in the wars of Biblical times, proud in his chariot, facing the Philistines.

This was the man who lingered in a farmhouse north of the Appomattox River Valley where a few guns still slammed in the night.

His enemy had already gone to rest in the Farmville Hotel. An aide escorted the tired General Grant to a poorly furnished room, the best the house afforded. An orderly went ahead carrying a candle.

"This room, sir," whispered the officer in an awed voice, as Grant sat on the bed and the orderly got down to help him off with his boots. "They tell me that General Lee slept in this same bed last night."

CHAPTER 3

WHITE FLAGS IN THE NIGHT

Sunday a soldier of Company A died and was buried. Everything went on as if nothing had happened, for death is so common that little sentiment is wasted. It is not like a death at home.

—Elisha Hunt Rhodes, 2nd Rhode Island Volunteer Infantry

ULYSSES GRANT LAY STARING INTO THE darkness. He thought about the note he had dispatched to General Lee late in the afternoon. He wondered how Lee would receive it, and what reply he would make.

There were several good reasons for Grant's opening a correspondence with his enemy on the subject of surrender. The previous evening he had talked to Dr. Smith, a relative of the famous General Richard Ewell, who with most of his command was now a prisoner of the Yankees. Ewell had told his doctor relative that he recognized the Confederate cause as lost.

Ewell felt that the Southern government should give in, and immediately, to prevent needless slaughter. He declared that it was little better than murder for soldiers to be killed as a strong army hammered at the flanks of a retreating host with no food in their bellies or in their haversacks and little prospect of securing any.

"Someone will be held responsible for these needless deaths if we don't give up immediately!" Ewell had cried.

Grant turned this matter over in his mind. Ewell was no weakling, no skulking straggler. He was a brilliant general who had given his leg for his cause early in the war, and who refused to languish at home thereafter—preferring to fight on, to campaign boldly through dog-days and sleet, the battered wooden leg sticking out from his stirrup as he rode.

If heroes like "Dear Dick" Ewell were ready to quit, Grant felt that he should give them the opportunity.

And more news had come to him as well: good news for the Northerners, dreadful news for the Secesh when they found it out. Large quantities of rations (food for at least eighty thousand men, it was believed) had been sent to meet Lee's army in its flight to the west. Trains loaded with grain, flour, meat, and other articles craved by hungry soldiers, were nearing a railroad village then called Nebraska Station, not far from Appomattox Court House. (Nebraska Station is called Appomattox nowadays.)

Sheridan, Grant's intrepid cavalry leader, was pressing close with his mounted columns. He sent word to his commander that he thought he could fight his way to Nebraska Station and seize the trains of provisions before Lee's starving fugitives could get their hands on them. Sheridan hadn't captured the food yet, but he said that he *expected* to seize it; that was enough for Grant.

An old man sat on the steps of the Confederate Soldiers' Home in Richmond and worked his toothless jaws. . . . "Food?" he repeated. "We didn't have no fit food. Some of us had a little corn—hard corn, flint corn—like you feed to hogs. Ever try to chew anything like that? Like chewing rocks . . . our gums were sore and bleeding."

When generals exchange letters, whether they are friendly generals or enemy generals, the letters are written in a very stiff form. The manner of writing is so complicated and there are so many long words that it is sometimes difficult even for the general who receives the letter to tell exactly what is meant until he has read it two or three times!

Let us cut through the high-sounding phrases, let us simplify them, and witness the thought actually conveyed in these notes.

April 7th, 1865

General R. E. Lee
Commanding C. S. A.
General:

You are beaten. Brave and determined as you are, there is no sense in your fighting longer against such odds. I think it is my duty to let you surrender your army peaceably if you will. Let us stop all this senseless killing.

U. S. GRANT, Lieutenant General

This message was carried under a flag of truce through the lines before it was quite dark . . . men in blue uniforms galloping close, waving their white flag . . . crouching Confederates lowering their guns . . . a few men in gray inching out suspiciously . . . the momentary contact, with all eyes turned upon the mingled foes; the folded paper passed from gloved hand to gloved hand; perhaps even a courteous salute given and returned; probably a grin and a wisecrack to cover the emotion of the meeting . . . the two parties separating, turning, galloping back to their own positions. . . .

The message was relayed from hand to hand, from officer to officer. Before ten p.m., hooves pounded up a lane to the farm where Lee was resting. The challenge, the muttered explanation, the frayed folded paper again, the rap at the door. . . .

General Lee was conferring with General Longstreet, one of his most able followers. Lee received the note, opened it himself, and held it close to the lamp. The expression of his face did not change. Without a word he passed the paper to Longstreet for him to read. Longstreet read it and handed it back.

"Not yet," he said, seeming to realize that his chief would refuse to surrender at the first demand.

Lee was reluctant to act immediately. For some weeks now he had been supreme commander of all the Confederate armies fighting against the North. Was Grant aware of this? Couldn't there be arranged a general treaty of peace, covering perhaps not only those thousands of tired men who still rallied under the eye of their gray-bearded boss in Virginia, but also those other thousands?

What about Johnston, in Carolina? What about Dick Taylor down south, and Kirby Smith, away out west across the Mississippi?

What terms, what terms? What could be arranged?

This query forced itself again and again through Lee's mind as he sat in the rustic parlor. He said nothing to his staff; probably he wished to take no one into his confidence. It would not do, if indeed the fight was to go on, to have rumors of surrender sweeping among his regiments.

Lee produced a sheet of cheap note paper, very like the kind you buy now in little five- or ten-cent tablets at the corner store . . . blue lines ruled across the page. Lee wrote to Grant.

April 7th, 1865

General:

I do not quite agree with you that the Confederate cause is lost, or that there is nothing to be gained by our fighting on. But I agree with you in your wish to stop the needless killing of brave men. What terms will you give me if I agree to surrender?

R. E. Lee, General

An old friend lingered at an outpost in the darkness, waiting for Lee's reply. His name was Seth Williams. Long ago, when Lee had been superintendent at West Point, Seth Williams was his adjutant. (An adjutant assists a commanding general with his orders and communications.) Adjutant for Robert E. Lee, big, baldheaded Seth Williams had once been; but now he was adjutant for Lee's opponent, Ulysses S. Grant—who in those long ago days was a mere captain in the Fourth Regiment!

It was after midnight before Lee's reply reached that bleak hotel room in Farmville. Grant read it, and pondered again. It was too late now to respond. He would wait until the next morning, and again request his adjutant to deliver a note to the enemy lines.

April 8th, 1865

General R. E. Lee,
Commanding C. S. A.
General:

There is only one thing you have to do. Surrender your troops, with the agreement that they shall not fight us any more. I will be glad to meet you any place you say, or I will send officers to meet any officers sent by you, to arrange this matter.

U. S. Grant, Lieutenant General

The hotel proprietor was on hand to greet his famous guest when the general came out, that Saturday morning, to ride along with his army. Strangely enough this proprietor had not been there the night before; but here he was now, and he wore a shabby uniform which showed that he was a colonel in the Rebel army, or at least had been.

He looked very hungry; probably his empty stomach was cutting a few capers as he scented the simple breakfast the Yankees prepared.

"Yes, sir, this is my hotel. I was colonel of a regiment raised in this neighborhood. But when we retreated past here I discovered that I was the only one left of the regiment! It had just crumbled to pieces; all the surviving men had gone home. General, may I surrender myself? There's nothing else to do."

"Stay right here," Grant told him. "I don't think anyone will bother you."

He knew that this crumbling process was going on all over the region. Apparently some of the troops were acting with a wisdom greater than that of their commanders . . . but if there were just some way to stop the killing!

There wasn't. Many more boys on both sides would lose their lives today.

CHAPTER 4

ACHING SOUL AND ACHING HEAD

Two Confederate armies Grant had captured entire, in this war and now the third and greatest of them was stricken, limping pathetically in its efforts to get away from him.

—Bruce Catton, *The Army of the Potomac: A Stillness at Appomattox*

THE SUN SHONE WARM AND YELLOW, AS IF trying to soothe the Army of Northern Virginia into forgetting its jumbled-up misery. A lot of rain had fallen a few days before; most of the roads were mushy quagmires. Teams of horses and mules floundered in the horrid soupy mud; they were as gaunt-ribbed as the men who tried to drive them.

Neither soldiers nor animals had been fed properly in a long time. Disease and weakness were claiming them. Wagons, cannon, caissons—the little ammunition carts so necessary to serve the old-fashioned guns—these were abandoned each hour. Sometimes they could be drawn off to the side of the road, to give the fleeing troops more room.

Sometimes, sadly enough, the animals collapsed in their struggle to drag the heavy vehicles out of the bog. They fell in their harnesses and lay waiting for death, bodies shuddering, swollen eyes glazing. If beasts could not survive this ordeal, what of the starved boys and men?

For a moment, however, the Confederates seemed to be outdistancing their pursuers. Many portions of the army had traveled at night. Thus, on Saturday they were not too severely punished by volleys from the Yankees clinging along the rear and flanks of the runaway columns.

It was quiet now for an hour or two at a time: no bullets whining overhead, no spatter of revolvers along intersecting roads.

General Lee had not caught much sleep the night before. Along toward noon he lay down on a blanket to rest. He was dozing briefly when an aide approached. One of his generals, said the aide—General Pendleton—wished to speak to the commanding officer. Lee arose to greet his visitor.

(Lee was forever a model of courtesy. He found it

difficult to shout at anyone, even when an officer deserved vigorous upbraiding. Seldom would he speak of or to his leaders in any but the most formal terms. He did not call them "Dick" or "Pete" as another less mannerly commander might. With dignity he called them "General Ewell" and "General Longstreet.")

Pendleton—he was in charge of the Confederate artillery—was acting as a spokesman for a number of the lesser generals who had discussed the situation. They had reached the conclusion that there was nothing left to do but surrender.

They wanted to make this first move, in order to save their chief the embarrassment of admitting his own defeat. Needless to say, Pendleton and the rest knew nothing of the note Lee had received from Grant the night before, and it seems that Lee had taken pains to make sure that they did not learn of it. Perhaps that is why he wrote his reply in his own handwriting, not trusting even his military secretary.

Men were leaving the retreat, wandering off to their homes as the Farmville hotel proprietor had done. They were drifting loose by the dozens and hundreds. If it became common knowledge throughout the

Southern army that General Grant had opened the way for a complete surrender, General Lee might possibly find himself with no army to surrender at all!

He was proud. He was a lifetime veteran, devoted to whatever cause he served. He had fought Mexicans, Indians, and Yankees, shrewdly and with heroism. It was against the grain of his nature even to entertain the notion of surrender, unless there could be no other notion to entertain.

Lee told Pendleton with feeling: "We certainly have too many brave men to think of laying down our arms!" There was still a bare possibility of winning through to those trains of food at Nebraska Station.

But every road and lane was dotted with muddy gray hummocks, piles of rags, and thin flesh . . . exhausted soldiers, boys and old men alike with empty stomachs, who had fought back and who had plowed ahead through the mud day and night until their aching muscles refused to carry them farther. So they stumbled flat and slept . . . or dreamed prone and feverish, waiting, waiting: either for death, or for Yankees to take them prisoner. They were too crippled to care what happened.

The silver-bearded man, their stiff-backed leader, still had a sword in his soul.

"Indeed," he told the younger officer in conclusion, "we must all determine to die at our posts!"

The second letter sent by Grant had not yet reached Lee. It went through the lines before noon, but the couriers had difficulty in finding Lee. It was dark before the note overtook him Saturday evening—so dark that a colonel had to light a candle in order for his commander to unseal and read the paper.

No, no—not yet, not yet.

No surrender so complete! There might still be an opportunity to make terms for the other Confederate armies in the field. Lee wrote his second reply accordingly, and sent it away through the night.

Lee's soul ached.

Grant's head was a throbbing misery.

Nowadays we might call it migraine—one of those nerve-racking, bullying tortures that rule the whole body, that make the temples tender and the eyes dizzy. All afternoon, as he rode in the sun, Grant jolted in his agony.

He was not starved, but at least he and his staff had been eating scantily. They left their headquarters' wagons far behind during the week; they had no changes of clothing, no toilet articles. Grant did not even carry the sword which any commanding general always wore at his side in those days. The sword might not be useful in battle (though cavalry sabers still clanged and cut in occasional skirmishes) but a general's sword was an emblem—a signal of command—almost as important as the stars that gleamed within the metal braid of his shoulder straps.

Grant's staff maintained no mess, no cook, or food supply throughout this headlong pursuit. They were here and there, making contact with various corps and division commanders. They picked up coffee or crackers from other people's messes, wherever they might be able to find them. At night they had been sleeping on porches or in houses along the way.

To such a farmhouse, on this weary evening of Saturday, April eighth, General Grant and his military family turned for shelter. It was a big white house with a central hall running through it, and Grant managed to walk steadily into the living room across the hall. There he sat down on a couch and held his hands against his splitting head.

"General, you *must* have some treatment for that."

"It'll be all right," the General replied.

"No, sir. I'm going to find a surgeon—"

"They've tried. There isn't anything a surgeon can do for a head like this."

"At least, sir, they'll have some mustard here in this kitchen. Let me bathe your feet in mustard and hot water. I'm going to put some mustard plasters on your wrists and on your neck—"

(That sounds dreadful, doesn't it? It was a standard remedy in those days of home doctoring.)

The mustard foot-bath was heated up; plasters burned against Grant's skin. No relief came. It wasn't a case of going down to the corner drugstore for a tin of aspirin. There were no corner drugstores in this rough Virginia countryside. And aspirin was an undreamed remedy in the far undreamed future. . . .

Other officers bedded down on the floor in a room across the hall; occasionally someone stole in to see how the commander was making out.

He was lying on the sofa with a wet cloth on his head when Colonel Whittier arrived at midnight with Lee's second reply. Immediately the note was taken in to Grant.

April 8th, 1865

General:

Your note reached me this evening. You must be mistaken—I was not proposing to surrender the Army of Northern Virginia. I merely wanted to know what terms you offered. I do not believe it is yet necessary for me to surrender this army. Still, we all want peace . . . if your proposals might help to bring that about, I should like to meet with you. We can talk. What about ten o'clock tomorrow morning, on the old stage road near here, between the lines of our two armies?

R. E. LEE, General

This wasn't the answer which Grant had hoped to receive. It was too indefinite . . . this was still a lot of talk. Lee seemed to be reluctant to give up, to lay down his arms. Yet there was hope. Lee wanted peace, and he actually suggested a time and a place for meeting.

The matter was very delicate, and would have to be thought over thoroughly.

It's hard to think things over thoroughly—even matters not so important as this—when your head is killing you. Grant lay down on the sofa again and closed his eyes.

About four o'clock in the morning, Colonel Horace Porter slipped in to look after the General again. Grant was gone. Porter went searching out in the yard. There was Grant, pacing up and down through the moonlight, unable now even to lie down and try to rest.

"How's your head, sir?"

Grant replied frankly that he was in torment.

Some of the other officers came out, and together they persuaded their leader to let them take him over to General Meade's headquarters near by. There would be a fire, and probably some hot coffee . . . coffee might help the headache.

It did. Grant began to feel a little better as dawn approached, and he was able to send his reply to Lee.

April 9th, 1865

General:

I cannot make a peace treaty with you. Peace treaties are a matter for Nations themselves to decide—not for generals in the field. If you Southerners will give up this fight which has now become so hopeless, you will save thousands of human lives and hundreds of millions of dollars of property. I hope that we can come to some agreement without the loss of another life.

U. S. Grant, Lieutenant General

Then an officer said: "Sir, let us bring an ambulance around to the yard for you, before we start to move forward? It's got a canvas cover on . . . the sun was terribly hot yesterday and probably will be today. Your headache—"

"No, thanks. I'll go horseback."

CHAPTER 5

GRAY MAN, GRAY HEART, GRAY HORSE

We knew by our own aching hearts that [Lee's] was breaking. Yet he commanded himself, and stood calmly facing and discussing the long-dreaded inevitable.

—Richard Wheeler, *Witness to Appomattox*

THAT SAME MOON, PEERING CURIOUSLY AT General Grant as he walked about the farmhouse yard in pain, observed his enemy a few miles away enduring a spiritual torture infinitely worse.

Lee had camped in the woods only two miles from Appomattox Court House. Like the Federal commander, he and his staff were without wagons, but for a quite different reason. Yankee cavalry had pressed so furiously upon the columns a few days before that Lee's party was compelled to destroy or abandon the bulk of its baggage.

Naturally each man saved his best uniform to wear. Thus they were clad in elegance—most of them in handsome new uniforms—their very Sunday-go-to-meeting best, saved heretofore for important military ceremonies . . . saved—who knows?—perhaps for a victorious parade when the Northern hordes were finally driven from the "sacred soil."

They sat around a fire of fence rails; they had few blankets. During the night Lee instructed certain of his troops to try to cut their way through the Federal forces in the west. He was still holding to a forlorn hope that he might be able to swing aside, with the bulk of the divisions remaining to him, and join General Johnston at the head of another Confederate army, away to the southwest.

But this desperate attempt failed before dawn. Now a solid mass of Federals blocked the way beyond Appomattox. Lee was hemmed in.

Other suggestions were offered. Perhaps the regiments should dissolve completely, here and now, and try to slip off through the woods in order to avoid capture by the Yanks. As many as two-thirds of the Confederate troops, it was hoped, might in this way avoid the act of surrender. Eventually they could reassemble at some agreed place, and once more take the field against their enemies.

But Lee said No. He saw that if his men followed this

course they would be classified as guerrillas, as armed marauders. They would have to rob and steal in order to live. Far better, he was beginning to think, for them to proceed to their homes and again assume the care of their families. In April there was still time to put a crop into the soil, to grow food for their children that year. Maybe they could earn enough to buy clothing and medicines and things like that.

Empty pockets, empty wagons, empty barns, empty gardens: always the emptiness of the Defeated in a long-fought war. . . .

The general and his staff had breakfast. It wasn't ham and eggs, it wasn't sausage or omelette. They took their tin cups, they held them over the fire with a little water and corn meal mixed together. They warmed this stuff above the coals and drank it down. It was better fare than most of the Confederate soldiers were enjoying in the pink dawn of that Sunday!

It may have been that the sight and taste of this miserable breakfast gruel worked an effect on Lee more powerful than the persuasion of counsellors.

Nothing to eat, nothing to eat!

Thousands of his men were as devoted as fanatics. They would fight until their bullet pouches were empty, food or no food; they would club their guns and fight with the butts. They would hurl rocks, they would use their fists. Soldiers had done that at Lookout Mountain, and on Little Round Top at Gettysburg. They might battle now as primitive savages, here amid the ragged fields of Appomattox County; but nothing would be gained in the end except death amid the corn shucks and the pines.

Lee looked at his staff. “The only dignified course for me would be to go to General Grant and surrender myself.” Surrender at last! Now he had admitted and announced it.

Robert E. Lee rode out toward the old stage road, accompanied by a few of his officers and by a courier, Sergeant Tucker, holding a white flag on high. Gray-faced general, gray beard, gray uniform, a gray steed. He was riding Traveller, as he had ridden the mighty horse when they first retreated from Petersburg.

Have you ever seen a picture of Traveller? General Lee had many mounts during the war, but Traveller was king of them all. Richmond and Brown Roan were dead, now. Ajax and Lucy Long . . . campaigns were too irksome for them, the cry of bullets too frightening; the burst of shell fire had rent their nerves; they were worn out.

Old Traveller danced or galloped boldly to the last—

a deep-chested, iron-gray horse with black points (his mane and tail were very dark). He stood sixteen hands high, as horsemen say, which meant that he was a very tall animal. And, like Lee, he was born in Virginia. He was seven or eight years old but as alert as any colt. He, too, had gone without food when it was necessary. He had been thirsty and frightened, like any soldier.

Traveller hated to walk. He liked to move at a rapid trot and often would trot thirty miles on end, never halting in his pace. It took a strong man to ride him in comfort. Lee was strong.

"What's going on over there?"

The little group halted, examining the landscape warily. Something was moving beyond the trees: A thick line of dark-clad men sagged out across the meadow.

"Yankee skirmishers."

The Confederates lifted their reins and moved on with caution. Ahead of them the sun spangled on metal of a uniform or a polished weapon. Yankee skirmishers . . . would they shoot? The Confederates had only their swords and a few revolvers. They were no match for numerous squads of riflemen drifting across the fields ahead.

But still Lee must proceed to the place of meeting, if

indeed a meeting was to come about. The general gripped Traveller's rein tightly; he could not let him trot now. They went on with the feeling that enemies were already sighting their guns in that direction—perhaps drawing a bead on the tallest, the silver-bearded leader.

" . . . White flag, sir."

"Yes. It is moving forward."

The man in blue who approached them was a colonel named Whittier, and he was fetching the note Grant had written that morning. Colonel Marshall rode ahead of his commander to meet the Northerner; he saluted in silence; he took the envelope from Whittier and rode back to Lee.

Lee read the letter.

"Please take paper and pencil, Colonel Marshall," he said, and the secretary obeyed. Lee began to dictate his reply.

An officer in gray dashed around a bend in the road. He had only one arm; he rode a horse covered with foam, a beautiful horse with swollen eyes, a mare who had been driven beyond her strength. This man was Lieutenant Colonel John C. Haskell, commanding an artillery battalion. He had ridden with insane fury when ordered by General Longstreet to find his commander.

Haskell announced that a road had been discovered whereby the Confederate army could escape from the trap of the surrounding Federals . . . Lee merely shook his head. Either he did not believe the report (it soon turned out to be a false rumor), or else he did not think that such an attempt to escape would be successful.

He went on dictating.

April 9th, 1865

Lieutenant General U. S. Grant
Commanding U. S. Armies
General:

I was here on the picket line, hoping to meet you, when your note arrived. Please let me have an interview to discuss a possible surrender, as you suggested yesterday.

R. E. Lee, General

The mere sending of this message, however, did not solve any difficulties. Close beyond the plum trees was a throng of armed Union soldiers bent on making an attack.

Once his mind had been made up to surrender, Lee was determined to go whole-hog, to strive in every manner possible to prevent the loss of more lives.

These were General Meade's men who approached in blue; the austere Lee did not hesitate to beg for a truce.

"Please ask your commanding officer," he said to Colonel Whittier, "to have his men hold their fire. Can't we arrange a truce, until my letter reaches General Grant?"

Couriers loped back and forth on their horses. The blue line moved forward, halted again. The Northern commander didn't feel that he had any right to order a truce. He had been told to attack. He must be a good soldier and obey a command, whatever the consequences.

Lee's secretary had a sudden inspiration. "Tell your superior officer," he said to Whittier, "to read General Lee's letter to General Grant. Surely that will explain matters. It's senseless now to have another battle!"

Whittier rode off again to find General Meade.

None of the generals wished to fight a battle now, when peace seemed so close; and heaven knows that the soldiers in the ranks had no wish to slaughter their enemies needlessly, any more than they wished to be slaughtered themselves. Yet that is war: An order is given, a command goes forth; it is like a vast precise ugly machine being wound up and set in motion. Only the top man can apply the brakes.

Another flag of truce fluttered in the sun; more horsemen came from the Union lines. A demand was made, and not in writing: General Lee and his party must withdraw at once, they must ride out of the way. Otherwise they would be caught in the cross-fire between two armies.

Hastily an additional dispatch was dictated; Colonel Marshall's pencil rubbed in desperation. "Please stop the fighting," prayed General Lee to Grant, "until we have had our interview, until we have discussed the terms of surrender."

Still the Yankee lines came bristling forward. A last warning was sent: The Rebel general must leave immediately, the advance could not be stopped.

Apparently more lives were to be sacrificed, and in vain. Lee's heart was heavy as he turned Traveller's head toward the rear. He rode back through his own lines and halted with Longstreet's men, awaiting the crash of cannon and rifles which would usher in the attack.

"Here comes a white flag, sir!"

General Meade had agreed to the informal truce (though Meade apparently doubted that it was proper for him to order such an armistice). He suggested that Lee had better send a copy of the letter to Grant through some other part of the lines. Lee did so at once; in fact, he made it even stronger than anything he had written before. Again, he begged to discuss surrender terms.

The trouble with the whole thing was that General Grant was hard to find. He was on a different road from the one where some of his subordinates thought him to be. It was nearly twelve o'clock, noon, before Lee's first letter caught up with Grant, together with a note from Meade, saying that he had granted a brief truce.

In his saddle Grant read these notes. He dismounted, sat on the roadside grass, and scratched out a hasty reply to Lee. He told him that he had just received his letter and would push forward to the front at once in order to meet him.

Oh, yes—Grant had had his headache all morning, too; but most mysteriously the pain seemed gone the moment he held Lee's letter in his hands. Nowadays doctors have a lot of complicated terms for things like this: They talk about auto-suggestion, hypnosis, psychosomatics, and all sorts of weird things.

General Grant's own explanation cannot be improved upon. "I was still suffering with a sick headache. The instant I saw the contents of the note, I was cured."

CHAPTER 6

COMPANY AT THE McLEANS'

Many are the hearts that are weary tonight,
Wishing for the war to cease
Many are the hearts looking for the right
To see the dawn of peace.
Tenting tonight, tenting tonight,
Tenting on the old camp ground.

—Walter Kittredge

APPOMATTOX COURT HOUSE WAS ONLY A tiny place in those days and isn't much larger now. A country road ambles out of a low valley and bends across a wide flat ridge, past the court house and a few private homes. In 1865 there was a store operated by a man named Ragland, and a jail without any prisoners in it.

Beyond fields separated by decayed apple orchards and belts of fresh-leaved timberland, where birds were piping, lay the farmhouses of folks named Tibbs, Webb, LeGrand, Christian, and some more. And also the farm of Mr. Sweeny.

He was a skillful performer on the banjo, and he had a son who was an even more enthusiastic musician than he. One of General Lee's favorite commanders—the adored cavalry genius, Jeb Stuart—had a passion for banjo music. Through the early years of the war, until he died of pneumonia a few months before Stuart was killed in action, young Sweeny followed faithfully, whanging on his banjo whenever General Stuart asked him to, chanting "Peas, Peas, Eating Goober Peas," or the more sentimental strains of "Lorena," until Sweeny was a tradition through the whole Rebel army.

They had done more than merely sing and play, those folks from the little house down the Appomattox road. Banjos until that time had only four strings; but the Sweenys thought that with a fifth string added the banjo might make better music. They proved it by putting on the fifth string and working out a whole system of new chords. Thus, our common banjos have five strings today.

Appomattox Court House might have been famous only as the home of the Sweenys, if Sheridan's cavalry hadn't managed to bottle up Lee's retreating army on that April weekend.

Not far from the court house, built comfortably in a grove of locust trees, stood the red brick house occupied by Mr. Wilmer McLean and his family. Mr. McLean had not always lived there with his wife, with his children Willie and Nanny, and the other relatives and friends who sat sometimes around his big dinner table. He used to live up in northern Virginia, adjacent to a wayside railroad station called Manassas Junction, and near a creek with the peculiar name of Bull Run.

Nearly four years earlier, dwelling amid those faraway hills with his wife and babies, Mr. McLean had been appalled one day when cavalry dashed across his yard, when guns began to boom and shells sizzled overhead. The battle of Bull Run, as it is called in the North—or Manassas, as it is called in the South—was starting right there on Mr. McLean's own farm.

This was the first large-scale encounter of the War for Southern Independence. It was fought with fury all day long, until the Northern army fled in disorder, scooting east along the road to Washington. Some of the neighborhood civilians died during the battle, but fortunately none of the McLeans was hurt.

Mr. McLean was a man of peaceable disposition. He didn't like grape-shot in his currant bushes or bayonets flashing past his cow barn. He didn't enjoy thinking that his babies might be pierced by stray bullets.

"No more of this," said the McLeans. "We'll move. We'll go far away from this region and its battles."

So they moved. They moved to Appomattox Court House, one hundred and fifty miles away. The first battle of the war had begun on their farm. They never dreamed that the last act would take place in their sitting room.

On this Sunday morning of April 9th, 1865, Mr. McLean was on a quiet errand. No one seems to know just what he was doing, walking along the road near the courthouse. None of the history books tells. They simply say that he was *there* (and this author doesn't know, either, although he has been to Appomattox Court House, and once visited with an old lady who, when she was a girl, used to play hide-and-seek with Willie and Nanny McLean and with them picked violets from the grass in front of their brick house. Even this old lady didn't know just what Mr. McLean was doing, strolling abroad in the Sunday sunlight; so we shall have to guess).

Perhaps he was going over to the LeGrands to borrow a scythe. Perhaps he was going to ask Mr. Tibbs to help him with some planting during the week to come—if only the soldiers would move away! Perhaps he was merely prowling the road in deep suspicion, resentful of the presence of armed mounted men who seemed to have pursued him across forty-five months and eight counties, in order to ruin his corn again.

He came out from the village, and approaching up the clay road he saw five riders. Mr. McLean rubbed his eyes as he gazed. During the past twenty-four hours he had seen a great many troops, but always they had been of one breed or the other—either gray or blue. And this little cavalcade was mixed: Three were in Confederate gray, two were dressed in the dark uniform of the North.

Were some of these men prisoners of the others? Had the three Rebels, led obviously by the tall bearded man on the big gray horse, captured the other two; or in some miraculous manner had the two Yankees managed to seize three of the Secesh?

Prisoners? None of these men could be a prisoner. The two Southern officers had their swords; so did the Yankee officer. The sergeant in blue and the sergeant in butternut had their revolvers.

Although Wilmer McLean did not yet know it, the two Federals were General Grant's aide, Lieutenant-Colonel O. E. Babcock, and his orderly. It was Babcock whom Grant had sent hastening to the lines with his last letter to General Lee, informing Lee that he had finally received his note at 11:50 a.m., and that he was pushing to the front to meet him.

Realizing that one well-mounted aide with his orderly could make better time than an entire staff, Grant told Babcock to gallop ahead. The colonel had done so; he had penetrated safely through the lines, and had found Lee sitting under an apple tree by the roadside.

No guns were popping anywhere in the distance. The two widespread armies seemed to squat sullenly, rifles ready, gazing at each other with dogged weariness, ready to fight again at the drop of a hat. Most of them were praying in their hearts that they would not have to fight.

A house, a house. Some place was needed for the meeting. A conference could not be held with convenience out-of-doors. There were no tents, not even a camp stool, and Lee had been reclining merely on a blanket spread over some fence rails beneath the tree. There would be long discussions, terms to be submitted and agreed to; ink and paper would be essential.

A house. . . .

Colonel Marshall, a grave bespectacled man with a Van Dyke beard, edged his horse close to the farmer who stared from the roadside. He told him in a low tone that the tall silver-haired officer was General Lee, that an important discussion was about to take place. Couldn't some dwelling in the vicinity be made available?

Mr. McLean hastened back up the road, keeping pace with Colonel Marshall as the secretary walked his horse. The others followed at a distance.

Here was a house; this might do. It was only a little place. Wilmer McLean did not know much about generals or their needs. In his ears still echoed the screeching volleys of long-ago Manassas. He was praying merely that no such volleys would be fired now.

Colonel Marshall dismounted and followed the farmer through a sagging doorway. He glanced around with disapproval. This was no fit place. The house was vacant; it was dirty as well. Leaves had blown in upon the winter winds; damp paper hung peeling from soggy walls; there were only a few boxes and sticks of furniture scattered about. It was a filthy place, all in all, and they could hear squirrels or rats scampering overhead beneath the shingles.

"This won't do," said Colonel Marshall sharply. "There must be a better house in this village."

Mr. McLean gulped and stammered. There was his

own house; it was just up the road a piece. He guessed maybe that was the best place around there.

Marshall inclined his head. "Thank you. Will you conduct us there, please?"

The party continued along the road. The court house came in view, then McLean's home. He pointed it out—snug behind its yard. Violets grew among old bricks at the stepside.

He led on through the carriage gate. Horses halted. The riders swung to the ground. Bridles were given into the orderly's hands. Mr. McLean vanished in nervous haste to make sure that his family was out of the way.

You may have heard of The Last Mile which condemned prisoners are supposed to walk, as they march from their cells to the place of execution. Some such feeling of hopeless doom must have filled the heart of Robert E. Lee as he saw Sergeant Tucker beginning to remove Traveller's bridle to let him nibble the grass.

Lee turned away and moved in silence up seven wide steps that led to the porch. Blue and gray, two other figures followed him: Colonel Babcock, the Northern aide, and Lee's own secretary, Colonel Marshall. Babcock's orderly was out in the highway, responding to a whispered order from his superior. He was to wait there, mounted, in the road, so that he could easily be seen by General Grant and could direct the general to the place of meeting.

Lee entered the hall and turned through a doorway at his left. He stepped into the McLeans' parlor, a room that ran the width of the house. It had one good-sized window at the front and one at the rear. A second door opened into the hall. The furniture was stiff and ornate, as was the custom in well-run country houses of the region: a fireplace with a clock on the mantel, a wide old sofa, tables . . . a few chairs were scattered about.

General Lee walked directly to a chair placed beside a small table near the front window. He sat down in silence, and put his hat and his gray gauntlets on the oval-topped table near him.

Colonel Babcock and Colonel Marshall could not speak. The power of casual conversation was gone, in a time like this. Here they were—sworn enemies—veterans of the long and bitter conflict.

Those thousands of other men in dun-colored rags or dirty blue uniforms were veterans, too: the men who leaned against muddy wheels of their cannons on a ridge west of the court house; the boys who prowled on their horses, peering narrow-eyed toward opposing lines; the worn-out infantry in damp grass, staring at the sky . . . waiting.

The house had been found. One general was already in it.

The two attendant colonels moved their feet . . . their boots squeaked . . . there was no other sound. Out in the yard a fly alighted on Traveller's sensitive ear. There sounded a jangle of accoutrements as the horse shook himself and then went on chewing the soft grass.

CHAPTER 7

THE GENERAL SAYS COME IN

One of Ord's soldiers wrote that the army should have gone wild with joy, then and there; and, he said, somehow they did not.

—Bruce Catton, *The Army of the Potomac: A Stillness at Appomattox*

ABOUT THE TIME COLONEL BABCOCK FOUND General Lee sitting under the apple tree, and while Marshall and Mr. McLean were searching for a suitable meeting-place, General Grant and his staff rode at a trot toward Appomattox Court House.

The road ahead of them was crowded with familiar, dirty, canvas-covered wagons; with other mounted men and files of foot-soldiers still advancing toward the front lines. Grant's party left the road and proceeded across open fields.

"What's that ahead, General?"

"Looks like Secesh to me," someone else said.

Field-glasses were brought out; everybody had a

good look. They saw well-armed folks in butternut uniforms. This was still a war, no matter who planned surrender! If Grant and his people continued on west, they would soon be among embattled Confederates who might not recognize the armistice proclaimed at other points.

Here was the Union commander-in-chief speeding foward to accept, as he hoped, Lee's surrender. Suppose that he became a prisoner of Lee's troops instead?

All hands considered it prudent to alter their direction and proceed to the court house by a roundabout route. It was nearly half an hour after Lee had entered the McLean house, before Grant came jingling along past Ragland's store.

He met General Phil Sheridan and a group of others in the road. Grant pointed, knowing that the Southern general must be awaiting him near by. "Is Lee over there?"

Sheridan's stern face relaxed in a smile. "Yes, sir. In that brick house."

No one else spoke for a moment. Grant said quietly, "Well, then, we'll go over."

He touched the reins; his big dark horse, Cincinnati, moved ahead. His staff followed—squeak of stirrups, crush of saddle leather, click and tinkle of rings and bridlechains.

They could see Babcock's orderly. He was sitting his horse where he had been told to wait, out in the road in front of the trees. He saluted . . . yes, Lee and Babcock were in that house.

The Federals turned in at the gate. In the yard Sergeant Tucker still guarded riderless horses. Contentedly they cropped the grass, knowing nothing of the strange get-together in which these humans were taking part.

Traveller was noted among Unionists as well as Rebs. Horses were identified closely in those days with the commanders who rode them.

(Little Sorrel, Stonewall Jackson's horse. He lived long after the war, grazing placidly in a field adjacent to the Soldiers' Home at Richmond. In death he stands in the museum, ears lifted quizzically, sun coming through panes of glass to gild his brownish coat. He seems awaiting forever the approach of his fabled leader, the weight on the stirrup that would come if his master lifted a boot and prepared to mount.)

Traveller's fame had reached even the ears of U. S. Grant. The rugged, iron-gray animal had carried Lee through the hard battles of 1862. He had waited beneath his majestic rider on the western ridge at Gettysburg, watching Longstreet's broken divisions stumbling back from the Union left center. He had passed through thickets of the wilderness; his meaty brain knew the grumble of brass cannon, the squeal of minie balls.

Cincinnati, ridden by Grant on this historic April Sunday, was only one of the handsome animals the Union commander owned during the war. There was the beautiful cream-colored stallion, Jack; and another brave horse killed at the battle of Belmont, early in the war—shot to death even while Grant was in the saddle!

Fox and Kangaroo . . . one a beautiful roan, the other a raw-boned creature abandoned by the Confederates at the battle of Shiloh, and fed and cared for attentively by Grant, his captor, until Kangaroo grew to be a very fine horse indeed. The string even included a pony named Jeff Davis, in honor of the Confederate President.

Just as Traveller was the prize of Robert E. Lee's stud, so the huge speedy Cincinnati was the gem of all the Yankee commander's horses. He was taller than Traveller, and famed as the son of a racehorse named Lexington—a fleet-footed beast who could run four miles in seven and one-third minutes (not fast, when you think of automobiles or jet bombers; but very fast for a horse—any time, any place).

People had offered Grant as much as ten thousand dollars for Cincinnati, but Grant refused to sell. He let very few people beside himself ever ride Cincinnati.

One of the exceptions was a raw-boned, dark-clad man with a sad face: a man who spoke slowly in a high-pitched voice, and who came to visit Grant the day after the capture of Petersburg. Poor gaunt-faced, sad-eyed rider . . . Grant's guest . . . and sitting well the satiny horse, for all his awkwardness! He didn't know that he had less than two weeks of life left to him.

It must have given the watching soldiers a thrill to observe the approach of Cincinnati, and see—not Grant, astride the beautiful horse—but Abraham Lincoln instead.

This was one other thing Lee and Grant had in common: both loved horses, both were magnificent riders.

There in the McLean yard, Grant dismounted and climbed the same seven steps his enemy had climbed a little time before. He wore no uniform of fine cloth, spotless and untarnished; his boots were battered, leather and trousers splashed with the mud of his riding. Clothing—a uniform—things like that didn't matter.

Nothing mattered except the business at hand. It was four years this month since guns at Charleston first spurted their flame against Fort Sumter. Bones of the dead lay in a thousand cotton fields, under ten thousand oaks and pines and sweet gum trees, from Texas to Florida, from Pennsylvania to Missouri and back again. Would this be the end of the killing?

The rest of the officers halted in the front yard; they let their chief go on alone. Through the window of the left-hand room Colonel Babcock saw him approaching, and went to open the door. The staff waited, with Traveller and the solemn sergeant in gray; they stood amid violets. Locust trees . . . a dove was crying its Sunday cooing song, and there were little wooden toys which the McLean children had been playing with.

Generals Sheridan and Ord had followed Grant down the road, with others. They halted, scarcely muttering to each other. Their eyes were on that brick house with its wide veranda—a simple dwelling become suddenly the focal point, the hub, the quivering heart of a stormy, disunited nation.

There was the sound of a door opening again. Colonel Babcock stood at the front entrance with his hat in his hand.

He gestured toward the sitting room. His voice was audible to the attentive blue-clad men in the yard. "The general says come in." They went.

More than a dozen officers were in the crowd, including those who had joined the party after they reached the court house. It was like entering a sick chamber, said Colonel Porter. They went in quietly, embarrassed, aware that their spurs and boots were making too much noise.

The room reeked with an atmosphere of tension and pity; the very walls were too silent. These men had fought with their nerves and bodies and minds, just as toughly as Lee and the Confederates had fought. Suddenly, in a wayside farmhouse, the weight was about to be lifted from their shoulders.

Or was it? Would the two commanders be able to agree on terms? Might not Grant again demand the same sort of surrender for which he had declared in long-ago Tennessee? It had won him the uncompromising nickname of "Unconditional Surrender" throughout the North.

He was sitting about ten feet away from Lee, beside a marble-topped table in the middle of the room. Like Lee, he had put his hat and gloves beside him.

Yes, he had a hat and gloves, but no sword. He was dressed in a private's uniform except for the authority depicted in stars on his shoulders. Lee, in stern and elegant resignation near the front window, looked like a prince in contrast.

More than that . . . a memory came to Grant. The war with Mexico, and General Scott commanding—oh, long, long ago!

Brevet-Captain Grant had been sent on an errand to headquarters. He went in the clothes he was wearing, an ordinary fatigue uniform which we would call Class B nowadays. He had paid no attention to the stilted order that all officers must appear at headquarters in full dress outfits. So he had gone, rumpled and dusty, and had reported to General Scott's Chief of Staff. . . . Business of the errand was attended to; the brevet-captain prepared to take his departure.

Across from him stood the severe figure of the Chief of Staff, splendid in the gilded epaulets of old-fashioned ornate full dress.

"I feel it my duty, Captain," said Colonel Robert E. Lee, "to call your attention to the order that an officer reporting at headquarters should be in full uniform!"

Did Lee remember that incident? Might he not now feel that Grant was guilty of deliberate discourtesy in not tidying himself up as a gesture to a defeated foe?

Grant cleared his throat. "I met you once before, General Lee, in Mexico. I think I should have recognized you anywhere."

Lee said politely, "I know I met you. I have often thought of it, and tried to recollect how you looked; but I have never been able to recall a single feature."

Some people might have been offended by a statement like this. Not Grant. He knew that in the army of the 1840s Colonel Lee was an admired figure of accomplishment and importance. Captains like himself—they were as common as horse-pistols.

Almost with relish Grant went on to talk about the war in Mexico. He wrote later, with honesty, "Our conversation grew so pleasant that I almost forgot the object of our meeting."

But Lee brought him back in a hurry. "I suppose, General Grant," he said, or words to that effect, "that you know why I am here. I came to find out about terms."

"Well, General, I propose just about the same terms

I mentioned in my letter yesterday. Your soldiers would be surrendered and then paroled until properly exchanged. They wouldn't be imprisoned. All your arms, ammunition, and supplies you would give to us."

Lee said that those were about the conditions he had expected. "General Grant, apparently we understand each other. I suggest that you put the terms on paper."

Grant asked for one of his staff to hand him his manifold order book. This was a tablet prepared with carbon paper, so that extra copies of the writing were made whenever a pencil was traced across the top sheet.

"Very well, I'll write out the terms." He opened the book on the table and set to work.

CHAPTER 8

HORSES, MULES, AND A SWORD

The full ranks will be shattered,
And the bright arms will be battered,
And the battle-standards tattered,
When the boys come home.

—John Hay

GENERAL GRANT WAS A HEAVY SMOKER; more often than not he preferred cigars. No one smoked cigarettes back in Civil War times—it is unlikely that most of the warriors had ever seen a cigarette!

On this occasion Grant had his pipe with him. He filled and lighted it before he began to write; he puffed steadily while he went about the business of composition and decision. Maybe he had known what he would write, all along.

Just as we dispensed with fancy words when reviewing notes exchanged before the actual surrender, so let us now put the actual surrender terms into a simple form, as well as the conversation which occurred.

Grant scribbled rapidly with his pencil. He wrote the details in the form of a letter to General Lee, date-lining it at Appomattox Court House, Virginia, April 9th, 1865. He said that he would receive the surrender of the Army of Northern Virginia on the following terms:

(1) Each officer must individually give a parole that he would not take up arms against the government of the United States until he was properly exchanged.
(2) Each company or regimental commander was likewise to sign a parole for the men under his command.
(3) All guns, cannon, and other public property possessed by the Rebels must be turned over to the Federals.

Momentarily the general stopped writing. His glance was resting, not on the proud hurt face of his defeated enemy, but on the beautiful sword at General Lee's side. It was a gorgeous piece of cutlery, with an ornamented hilt. If the sword had been drawn from its scabbard, all eyes might have seen that the gleaming steel blade was beautifully chased with designs and inscriptions.

Union officers in the room thought that this must be the fabled sword of fantastic workmanship which was presented to Lee by his native state of Virginia. This was not quite the case; it was a ceremonial weapon which Lee called his "Maryland sword." Today it can be seen at the Confederate Museum in Richmond.

From time immemorial it had been the custom for a surrendering commander to deliver up his sword to the victor. Lord Cornwallis did that, when he surrendered to the American Revolutionary Army at Yorktown (except that Cornwallis did not have the nerve to face the American commander in person! He sent an officer to represent him and hand over the sword in his stead).

No one will ever know exactly what went on in Grant's head at this moment. He was not given to lengthy discussion of his innermost thoughts. He says in his memoirs merely that it would have been "an unnecessary humiliation" to compel Lee to engage in this sad ceremony.

Therefore he wrote: "These surrender terms do not mean that the officers have to give up their side-arms or their own horses and personal baggage."

Grant concluded the letter speedily. He wrote that if

these conditions were agreed upon, all the Confederates could return peaceably to their homes and would not be disturbed further if they were law-abiding and observed the paroles granted them.

A secretary, Colonel Ely S. Parker, was motioned over to Grant's chair. He stood at his shoulder, re-reading the terms the supreme commander had written down. There was a low murmur of voices repeating a phrase or two . . . no one else could make out just what was being read or said. Under his chief's direction, Parker wrote in several words and made a few minor corrections.

Ulysses S. Grant arose, walked deliberately over to Lee, and put the manifold order book into the Confederate's hands.

"Will you read this, General Lee, and see if it covers the matter fully?" Grant returned to his own chair.

When hours are most tense, when pressure seems straining us to the utmost, we human beings do many little mechanical things in order to ease the burden on our souls. The accused prisoner plays with a torn cigarette stub or with the tip of his own necktie while he is being questioned by the police. A salesman, sitting in an outer office, wondering about the acceptance or the rejection of the big order on which he has pinned his hope . . . he bends a paper clip into a figure-8 and straightens it out again.

So General Lee tried to control himself now. He put the order book on the table; he fumbled in his pocket and found his spectacle case; he drew out his handkerchief and proceeded to wipe his glasses with care, shining each lens.

At last he managed to cross his legs and anchor the spectacles across the bridge of his nose. At last he took up the book and read the terms.

In the second long sentence, General Grant had omitted a word. Even Colonel Parker had not observed the mistake when he re-read the material. This was in the top line on the second page.

Lee lifted his gaze and looked across at the Northern general. "After the words 'until properly' the word 'exchanged' seems to be omitted. You doubtless intended to use that word?"

Grant nodded. "I thought I had put it in."

"No, I guess you left it out by accident. Shall I write it in?"

"Certainly."

Lee searched his pockets for a pencil; he had none. A

Northern colonel, Horace Porter, was standing nearby, and quickly he offered a pencil of his own to Lee. Lee inserted the word "exchanged."

(You can see it in his own handwriting, in the photographed reproduction of the surrender letter, if you should chance to examine Volume Two of Grant's Memoirs. All the handwriting . . . Grant's own loose sprawling script, the neater blacker words inserted by Colonel Parker, and finally the one word put in by Lee with the "ex" well separated from the "changed.")

There should be a reverence in the attitude with which any student approaches an examination of this facsimile. Here is reproduced the smeared, heart-breaking finale of America's most tragic internal chapter . . . black scribbling . . . two of the greatest Americans of their time, and all the force and agony they commanded, reduced to a mere scratching on a yellow page.

Lee finished reading. He removed his glasses and looked across at the man who had conquered him. He could not bring himself to mention it—yet he was keenly grateful for the generosity displayed. No shackles, no prison bars, no dismal yielding up of treasured, useless swords!

He said, with the first real warmth he had shown during the interview, "This will have a very happy effect on my army!"

Grant's eyes flickered. "Very well, General. Unless you have some other suggestion, I'll have a copy of this letter drafted immediately in pen and ink."

Lee didn't say anything for a moment. Then—"There's just one thing I'd like to mention, General Grant. In our army, unlike the way it is in yours, soldiers of the cavalry and artillery own their own horses. Will my men be able to keep their horses, and not surrender them?"

Grant gazed squarely at Lee. "I'm afraid you'll find it isn't stated that way. Only officers may take their private property home with them."

Lee looked at the letter again. He knew the horrible conditions all over the South . . . no horses, no mules anywhere. He hadn't been able, for a long time, to find sufficient animals to serve the needs of his army. The majority of Southern farms had no stock left on them.

Spring . . . greenness and violets outside . . . fresh tiny leaves of the locust trees bore witness to the season. So did the wet clay soil, and the birds scampering to hunt for worms.

This was a time for plowing and seeding. But how

could Lee's beaten soldiers, turned into peaceable farmers once more, plant their cotton and tobacco? How could they plow up the weeds, that strangled corn and sweet potatoes, if they had no animals to help their cultivation?

Lee did not beg further. All he could say was: "No, I see the terms would not allow my men to retain their animals; that is very clear."

He waited for Grant's reply. Other people, standing stiff and silent in that room as they had stood for nearly an hour—they waited also. So did the world outside, and the years to come. They lingered to witness the generosity of this sober-faced harness-store clerk who had once been forced to resign from the Regular Army because he was considered unfit for his job—who had left California in disgrace the same year Robert E. Lee sat with cool pride in the superintendent's office at West Point.

Grant said: "Well, I didn't know that your private soldiers owned their own animals. I guess most of the men in your ranks have small farms. Your portion of the country has been so raided by the two armies . . . I think your men would have great difficulty in planting crops for their families. Suppose it's arranged in this way: I'll instruct my officers who receive your army's parole to let every man who claims to own a horse or mule take the animal home with him."

A warmth of thankfulness gushed in Lee's heart. It was a long moment before he could speak. "This will have the best possible effect upon my men! I believe it will go a long way toward healing the wounds of war."

Colonel Parker began to make a copy of the surrender letter in ink. He went to a third table at the rear of the room, to work. But wait—there was no inkwell handy.

An officer went to summon the owner of the house, Mr. McLean. McLean hastened away in a nervous flutter and came back with a cone-shaped inkstand of stoneware, but Colonel Parker found that the well was dry.

It remained for the defeated Confederates to produce this important necessity. Colonel Marshall promptly took from his pocket—no, not a fountain pen (it would be a long while before those were invented)—but a little portable inkwell. People used to carry things like that before the days of fountain pens. This one was made of boxwood—a tiny polished cylinder—two pieces of wood screwed tightly together around a glass inkwell in the middle.

With the aid of Rebel ink, Parker went ahead

copying Grant's letter. After that Colonel Marshall, at Lee's direction, wrote out a brief letter of reply consisting of only three sentences, and stating that General Grant's terms were accepted.

While this paperwork was being performed, Grant took advantage of the opportunity to introduce the various generals who had come into the room, together with members of his own staff, to General Lee. For the first time in years the bearded man in gray shook hands with his old friend and former adjutant, Seth Williams. It was Williams who had busied himself two days earlier in taking the first exchange of letters back and forth.

Lee greeted Williams warmly, but he was in no mood for social pleasantries—especially with strangers who had helped to batter his beloved army into defeat. When an officer extended his hand, Lee took it in a formal manner; to most of them he merely bowed.

It was only when Colonel Ely Parker was introduced to him that Lee showed a noticeable change in his manner. In slang we might call it a "double-take"! At fifty-eight Lee's eyesight was not of the best, and Parker had been across the room from him all this time. The Confederate had not realized that the colonel's heavy face was dark, that his hair and eyes were black as well.

How long do you suppose it was before Lee learned the truth: that Colonel Ely S. Parker was a full-blooded American Indian, and the reigning chief of the famous Six Nations far in the North!

CHAPTER 9

"TELL THEM TO STOP"

Now large numbers of rebel soldiers came over to us. We were glad to see them. They had fought bravely and were as glad as we that the war was over.

—Union Private Theodore Gerrish

BEHIND CONFEDERATE GUNS, FAR PAST THE thin-leaved trees and watching cavalry, there were more than a thousand men who would greet the news of surrender with wild enthusiasm.

They did not wear butternut rags; they were dressed in the clothing of Federals. They sat or lay on the ground or wandered idly in groups under the eyes of gray-clad guards with bayonets fixed to their muskets. Not all the prisoners captured during the concluding hours of this campaign were dog-tired Secessionists. These fellows were prisoners as well—Yankees gathered up by the hard-fighting Rebs in a score of major and minor affrays during the retreat.

They were on General Lee's mind now, as he turned from the frigid ordeal of introduction.

He spoke to Grant about these prisoners. "I'd like to send them into your lines as soon as possible. I have no food for them or for my own men. Most of my troops have been living on parched corn. I did telegraph to Lynchburg, asking for several train loads of rations to be sent to me on the railroad. As soon as they get here, may I have my men supplied with food?"

Every other eye in the room except Colonel Marshall's was turned instantly toward General Philip Sheridan. He knew what had happened to those carloads of food, and so did all the Union officers. Sheridan's cavalry had captured those trains the previous evening.

Let it be a further credit to the kindness of General Grant that he did not mention the fate of Lee's foodstuffs. Some conquerors might have cried bluntly, "Your rations are now in our hands!" Others might have tried to make a joke of it. Grant did neither.

He said, "Naturally, I'd like to have our own men returned to us right away. And I'll take steps at once to feed your army. How many soldiers do you have left?"

Lee shook his head. "I can't say. We've lost a great

many in killed and wounded, and there have been stragglers and deserters. All my reports and records had to be destroyed during the retreat, to keep your people from capturing them."

"Suppose I send over rations for twenty-five thousand men—will that be enough?"

"More than enough." Lee added with gratitude, "It will be a great relief to me, to know that my men are fed."

They were fed at once. For hours big wagons went rumbling past the hollow-eyed, tattered hosts in gray. Boxes, bales, sacks of grain—they were transported amid the surrendering regiments as speedily as teams could drag them there. The fields echoed to the wrenching sound of hatchets and bayonets tearing off the tops of hardtack boxes.

Lee had suggested—wisely, he seemed to think—that the two armies should be kept well apart for the time being. He appeared to fear that fights and riots might break out between men who had so bitterly engaged in mortal combat and for so long.

If such unpleasantness occurred, no one seems to have written about it. There may have been surly looks; certainly there were bitter hearts within the breasts of the beaten army. But past broken rail fences, through the pine fuzz, Yankees came creeping forward. They were curious to have a closer look at these dust-colored phantoms who had opposed them so staunchly on a hundred battlefields.

Haversacks were unbuttoned, misshapen tin cups were produced, knives went slicing into slabs of greasy pork. The Rebels gazed in starving disbelief.

"Here you be, Johnny."

Soon the beans bubbled in makeshift pots; the scent of scorched fat rose richly amid the haze of early evening. Food! It was strange for the Yankees to be meting out bread to these multitudes for whom they had reserved nothing choicer than lead bullets and cold steel since 1861.

Fires crackled as the sun went down, and on into the night, and through the damp dawn to come. Voices talked back and forth through the smoke.

"Were you there, too?"

"Yes, I was serving in the Thirteenth Virginia then."

"You must have been right opposite us. We captured a few fellows from the Thirteenth Virginia."

"Yes, suh, we lost a lot that day. Had a sight of men killed, too. That was mighty heavy fire you were throwing at us. . . ."

But in the McLean parlor, after more than two hours

of deliberation and discussion, there was still no hint of the brotherly reunion which would come in time. A few minor details were discussed; the letters of surrender and acceptance were signed by the two generals.

Robert E. Lee took up his gloves and his hat. Union officers stood aside in silence as Lee walked from the room with Colonel Marshall following him closely.

It was a little before four o'clock. Man after man, generals and subordinate staff officers edged through the hall and out to the wide front porch. Lee stood looking about for Traveller.

Several Federal junior officers, gathered on the porch to see and hear what they could of the momentous ceremony within, had leaped up when Lee appeared; they saluted the ex-foeman with proper respect. Lee put on his hat. He returned the Yankees' salute, scarcely seeming to see the young men as he did so.

He moved to the top of the steps and put on his riding gauntlets. He stared off across open lawns and meadows of the country village. Over there, past trees toward the north and west, his army was waiting. He must go to them with news he never thought he would have to bring.

He struck his gloved hands together several times, and those nearest him said that he seemed to utter a sound, a ghastly exclamation, a sad word given to himself alone. We will never know the word he spoke.

Then he seemed to come out of his stupor, and again searched the yard for his gray horse. No Traveller in sight, no Sergeant Tucker. The orderly had followed the grazing animal around the corner of the house, where General Lee could not see him.

Lee called out in a choking voice, "Orderly! Orderly!"

"Yes, sir." Tucker came, leading Traveller, and halted in front of the steps. The general walked down and waited while Tucker began to adjust the bridle which he had taken off.

"Lee himself," says Douglas Southall Freeman, his biographer, "drew the forelock from under the brow band and parted and smoothed it."

Many years later, fiddles were playing in the June night. Over near the Soldiers' Home a party of young folks danced to banjo music, and some of the shaggy gray veterans were dancing, too. Every now and then the distant strains of "Dixie" would rise from some other band; people would join vigorously in the Rebel Yell. An old man bent forward out of his chair, his cob pipe shaking in his withered hand. "I saw him," he whispered. "I was down there to Appomattox when it happened. Lee come toward us, riding on Traveller. His face—I tell you, it was the saddest face ever I see. He had the look of death on him."

Lee swung his long, strong leg over the saddle and adjusted his feet in the stirrups. Ulysses S. Grant stepped past his silent officers and moved down the porch stair. He walked slowly toward General Lee. He, too, had donned his hat when he came out of the house, but now he lifted it as he faced the man whom he had beaten.

Behind Grant, one by one, the other Yankees followed suit. There they stood, a ring of blue-clad conquerors bare-headed, gazing respectfully at the silver-bearded warrior whom they could not help but admire, much as they had loathed the cause for which he fought.

Robert E. Lee lifted his own hat in brief unspoken farewell. Then, staring blankly ahead of him, he turned Traveller toward the gate.

At that time the cost of maintaining the Northern armies in the field amounted to more than four million dollars per day. That was a tremendous outlay for the 1860s, when a dollar bought many times the value it buys now.

This terrible cost weighed heavily on Grant's mind. Certainly the other Federal forces in the south and southwest would have to be kept in operation until remaining Confederate commanders followed Lee's example in surrender. Oh, more angry skirmishes would be fought in the weeks that followed, though not by the men directly under Grant's command.

Johnston would continue his advance into North Carolina, with the persistent Sherman following him. Duke and Stoneman would snarl amid groves and crossroads as their cavalry squadrons met; Colt's revolvers would bang, boys would topple to the ground—Appomattox or no Appomattox. Wilson would lead his columns through eastern Alabama and into Georgia . . . powder smoke rolling high, the Rebel Yell soaring in the afternoon.

But at least the back of Confederate resistance was broken. By journeying to Washington as soon as he could, Grant might be able to arrange for the withdrawal and mustering out of his legions from the Virginia campaign. The total cost would be reduced, and quickly; he must prepare to bring about such reduction.

Grant did not linger in the McLean yard more than a few minutes after Lee had gone. His staff was directed to mount. They started for their headquarters camp, which had been pitched that afternoon not far from the court house.

Doubtless many of the men looked wistfully back at that brick house of the McLeans now grown famous. They thought of chairs and tables in the historic room—little odds-and-ends of family life sitting about—ornaments, pictures on the wall. They would have liked to secure some of these things to take home with them—to "liberate" them, as our modern soldiers said when they were gathering souvenirs in Germany! But there was no chance for this, not for the staff. They had to follow their chief.

Boom.

People glanced at the horizon. Surely those were cannon being fired. Had the war broken out all over again?

Boom. . . . Boom.

Grant turned to the man riding nearest him. "What's that?" Sound of the cannon continued.

The colonel said with a smile, "I guess it must be a celebration, General. Probably the good news has trickled over to our artillery, even in so short a time! The cannoneers are firing salutes in honor of victory—"

"Tell them to stop."

The staff looked at Grant in amazement.

"Send word at once," he said curtly. "Tell them to stop that firing. We must have no such celebration. The war is over, the Rebels are our fellow-countrymen again. The best rejoicing we can show would be to forget any such demonstration."

An aide went clattering off in response to this peremptory command. Within a few minutes the firing ceased, and there was only silence . . . clear conversation of bluebirds along the hedgerows, the distant blatting of a calf which had not been butchered for army meat and now would never be.

"General . . ."

Grant's weary eyes rested on his questioner.

"Have you forgotten something, sir? I don't believe you've yet informed Washington of what's happened down here."

General Grant nodded. He called for pencil and paper. He halted at the roadside, dismounted, and sat down on a big stone which bulged from the dusty grass.

Once more the terse harness-clerk from Galena began to scribble an historic message—this time a telegram—to be sent to the Secretary of War. "General Lee surrendered the Army of Northern Virginia this afternoon. . . ."

CHAPTER 10

TRAVELLER DID NOT UNDERSTAND

With malice toward none, with charity for all, with firmness in the right as God gives us to see the right, let us strive on to finish the work we are in, to bind up the nation's wounds . . .

—Abraham Lincoln

SOMEWHERE YOU MAY HAVE SEEN A CERTAIN peculiar old colored picture. There are thousands of copies of it, on walls all over the United States. It shows painted Indians, leaping and tussling with tomahawks in hand . . . the dust of hot plains rising around the crowd of Last Stand folks in cavalry pants who are selling their lives with smoking Winchesters! And—properly defiant, revolver in hand—General George Armstrong Custer, with the long locks and the fringed shirt, shooting down as many hideous foemen as possible before they rush in to scalp him.

But observe him as he appeared at the Appomattox surrender: twenty-five years old, blond and brawny, wearing a black velvet jacket adorned with crimson silk, and a flowing red necktie. It's true—general officers were permitted to design their own uniforms. Custer is the only Federal on record who went to such extravagant lengths in personal adornment.

He was there at the McLeans' with his boss men, Sheridan and Ord. He was the boy wizard, the prodigy of the Army of the Shenandoah, wherein he commanded the Third Division. He had a pretty young wife at home, and an ego as large as a cannon ball—this jaunty cavalry commander who was not too well liked by his own men. Pig-headedly he would dash the Seventh Cavalry and himself to bloody destruction at the Little Big Horn in distant Montana, before twelve more years had passed.

"Twenty dollars!" cried General Sheridan to Mr. Wilmer McLean.

The farmer rubbed the back of his head. He was nearly stupefied at what had taken place in his sitting room—at what was still taking place only a few minutes after the surrender.

"Twenty dollars—gold," snapped Sheridan. "That's a lot of money, Mister. I'll give it to you . . . sell me that little table where General Lee sat!"

McLean extended his palm feebly and Sheridan dumped in the gold coins. "Here you are, Custer," he cried, catching up the oval table with its four spool-spindle legs. "Present this to your charming wife with my compliments!"

Custer beamed his thanks. Jubilantly he swung the table over his shoulder and hustled out to his horse. He sprang into the saddle without touching the stirrup: He was proud of his horsemanship, and justly so. An orderly handed up the table. Custer's horse went dancing out into the road; the rider whooped his delight and his excitement, and the laughing dirty soldiers along the road yelled in response.

Mr. McLean's furniture and possessions seemed to be going the way of all such articles when they have been associated with a momentous hour of history. General Ord was paying him forty dollars for the larger table beside which General Grant had sat. (Later on he would present it to Mrs. Grant, but that lady would politely decline to accept this present. She insisted that General Ord's own wife should have the relic instead.)

Grant's staff was gone, but other generals were there. More people thronged in at the door every moment, crowding the hallways of the simple house, wandering along passages, peering into other rooms where the McLean family had sought refuge.

A big bearded colonel was taking down a picture with a heavy frame that hung in a rear corner of the room. The mantel clock was seized by a weather-tanned young captain. The bowl, the little blue bowl which had been sitting over there—what had happened to it? No one seemed to know. Shouting officers surrounded the bewildered McLean, crying aloud their bids, fairly tussling over the souvenirs.

Colonel Porter hints meaningly in his account of the surrender that some things were stolen by men who pushed their way into the sitting room. Mr. McLean may have found himself poorer in purse, if richer in pride, after the events of that afternoon!

Beyond rusty pines and tumbled fence rails where the Rebel army had hung silently waiting for news, there was no such jubilation. If rumors of the surrender reached Confederate ears in advance of the actual return of General Lee, they were disbelieved. Marse Robert was a pillar of fire, a symbol of strength as dauntless as the golden Virginia sun itself. In some way he *must* have averted disaster.

A truce? Oh, yes. . . . Surrender? His men could not believe it.

There would be reunions in the hours to follow. The two commanders would meet again on the tenth of April, before Grant left for Washington and before Lee began a slow sad trek to the Richmond house where his ailing wife awaited him.

The friendship between Seth Williams and Robert E. Lee was only one of thousands which had been temporarily cut short by the four-year conflict. Longstreet . . . it was fewer than seventeen years since he had been mere "Cousin James" to a certain pretty girl who was married one warm evening in St. Louis. Like all blushing wartime brides of whatever century, Julia Dent had thrilled at the homecoming of the brave young man to whom she was engaged.

When the brown-faced Captain Grant returned from Mexico in the summer of 1848, he did not know that many of those who frolicked with him and his bride would in time be opposing him fiercely in the field. One of Ulysses' old mess-mates was a captain named Cadmus Wilcox; Grant chose him to serve as groomsman.

Well, Cadmus Wilcox was at Appomattox today

also; but he was a downcast major-general in a gray uniform, and his heart was like lead in his breast.

Defeated Southerners would, many of them, rise nobly to the occasion. On Monday Gray and Blue would find their way again to the McLean house as a convenient rendezvous. There they would talk of boyish adventures at "The Point" and exploits together south of the border. Even the recent months would be mentioned—that evil period when in all honor they would necessarily have had to die or surrender themselves if they had met in person. Gordon, Heth, Pickett: They all had friends among these rejoicing Yankee circles. They would be able to smoke together and even laugh, because they had the intelligent power of gentlemen.

But such jollity, however forced and assumed, lay in the immediate future. There was nothing but heartache and shocked disbelief to greet Lee and Marshall as they rode down the ridge, over the valley, past their own pickets, and up amid knots of ragged survivors who awaited them.

Traveller alone did not understand.

The soldiers were watching him; that much he knew. He was a show horse, after a fashion, and forever keenly aware of the attention paid to his master and thus turned on Traveller himself. Times when the troops cheered Lee, the tall gray horse would acknowledge the enthusiasm by little tosses of his maned head. The soldiers had laughed often at this. They would cheer and cheer again, and each time Traveller would toss his head. The boys loved to see him do it.

Not now . . . not on this Sunday. . . . Lee had halted to confer with certain of his generals. There was the machinery of surrender to be set in motion, an arrangement about the giving of paroles.

It was nearly sunset when General Lee started toward the rear where his new headquarters had been established under the trees. A nervous, saddened army rushed to meet him.

They formed in a ragged wall crowding close on both sides of the road. More men trotted up, many galloped on horseback. Dirty bewhiskered groups gathered at the fence corners.

Surrender . . . doom . . . defeat. Many of the soldiers cursed venomously and aloud. Many merely stared with faces hard and set. Hundreds were sobbing like children.

"General, we can still lick those Yankees!" they had cried, when Lee first came into the lines. "You just say the word, and we'll fight them again!"

Traveller arched his handsome neck and pressed his big jaw more heavily against the bit. He was slowing his pace, he was compelled to slow down. These embittered waifs were increasing in number and they were coming closer.

Like the well-trained steed of a mounted policeman, Traveller picked his way carefully through a press of bodies to avoid stepping on people's feet. All very strange, he must have thought in his horsey brain . . . why were they around so close, so close? Why were warriors climbing rocks and fences, shoving and jostling as they wept?

Why the hard, thin hands clutching at stirrup leather, rubbing the general's boots with reverence . . . and fingers clawing at Traveller's very flanks and chest, fondling the iron gray of his satiny coat?

He blew a sudden spray from big dark lips, he came close to whinnying a query. Hands, hands, they were touching his mane, they were rubbing along his withers. Perhaps—he wondered—perhaps another battle was soon to come? The animal lifted his ears and rolled his eyes at the notion of it.

But there would be no more warfare, not for the Army of Northern Virginia. That army was ceasing to exist here and now.

Through their tears the men could still find voice to cheer their commander. A thin yell rose fiercely from the tattered ranks: "I love you just as well as ever, General Lee!"

No, Traveller could not understand . . . cheers. Ah, yes: The veteran horse knew what to do when he heard applauding cries, when he heard the name of *Lee*. He arched his neck, he stepped forward with delight and purpose . . . he must toss his head now. This was a great occasion, it seemed—men were cheering.

An awful rage still clung in human hearts. The original determination, the original belief—they were still to be reckoned with, no matter how many Northern volleys had pierced and shattered the gray regiments.

A man howled wildly (the general could hear him): "I wish every damn Yankee on earth was sunk ten miles in hell!"

More generations would need to live before the gaping wound of sectional cleavage was stitched together. Its scar would be there forever.

In time the body of the nation would be whole, though marked with the rough tissue of healing. Years of work and struggle lay ahead for the broken Rebels and for the men who had conquered them. Yes—and for their children and grandchildren to come; and for the great-grandchildren, perhaps, who would fight side by side at Iwo Jima and in the Bulge, and in the air above Berlin.

In 1950 two descendants of Grant and Lee would stand on that same Appomattox site. Their hands would touch and clasp . . . rosy Confederate battle flags rippling in harmony with the Stars and Stripes. But not this Sunday, not today.

Traveller did not realize what it was all about.

Lee saluted his tearful men in farewell; he walked silently into the tent which had been set up for him. Peace had come to the counties of Virginia, but there was a feeling of storm in the air. The next day it would be raining.

ABOUT THE AUTHOR

MacKinlay Kantor was born in Webster City, Iowa, in 1904. As a young boy he had a special interest in the Civil War and he spent hours sitting and listening to Civil War veterans. Kantor's mother was the editor of the *Webster City Daily News* and his writing career began when he won a statewide writing contest (using a pseudonym) for this newspaper when he was seventeen.

When Hollywood bought his best-selling novel *Long Remember,* Kantor moved to California to work as a screenwriter, but World War II soon cut short this career. As a war correspondent, he covered the air battles in Europe. In 1945, Kantor published *Glory for Me,* which became the Oscar-winning film *The Best Years of Our Lives.*

Ten years later his remarkable novel *Andersonville* was published. Kantor was awarded the Pulitzer Prize for this grimly realistic story about the infamous Confederate prisoner of war camp in the Civil War.

During the course of his career, MacKinlay Kantor published over thirty books and hundreds of short stories, essays, poems, and articles. His novels were frequently adapted for films and he even appeared as an actor in one.